The Four Channels of Confidence:

How to Cultivate and Radiate Self-assurance

Margo C. McClimans

Margo C. McClimans

Copyright © 2024 Margo C. McClimans

First Published in 2014

All rights reserved.

No part of this publication may be reproduced, distributed, or transmitted in any form or by any means, including photocopying, recording, or other electronic or mechanical methods, without the prior written permission of the publisher, except in the case of brief quotations embodied in critical reviews and certain other noncommercial uses permitted by copyright law. For permission requests, please contact Coaching Without Borders GmbH permissions@coachingwithoutborders.com

The use of this work in whole or in part by automated processes or devices such as AI-driven content generation, aggregation, summarization, or translation is expressly prohibited without the written consent of the author and publisher. Unauthorized reproduction or distribution of this work, or any portion of it, may be subject to prosecution.

ISBN-13: 979-8-8664-9795-9

DEDICATION

This book is dedicated to my dear friends and loving family. You've seen me at all my highs and lows and love me anyway.
I am the luckiest girl in the world!

Margo C. McClimans

CONTENTS

	Introduction	1
	Stages of Confidence	5
	What is Confidence?	9
1	The Breath Channel	13
2	The Attitude Channel	23
3	The Voice Channel	53
4	The Body Channel	63
	Multiplying Your Confidence Through Relationships	79
	Final Visualization and Reflection	83
	Action Plan	87
	References	89
	About the Author	93

PREFACE TO THE SECOND EDITION

A lot has happened since the first edition was published in 2014. I have come together with the man of my dreams, and together we have expanded his incredible family with our precious son. Living as a Mom, "bonus mom", and life partner has helped me grow and changed me in many ways. And, it has tested and helped build my confidence over and over!

Moreover, this second edition was written after the advent of Artificial Intelligence and Large Language Models. I am proud to say every word was written by me and not AI.

INTRODUCTION

Many people have asked me why I wrote this book for women. In my coaching practice, I have a particular passion for working with women and gender-diverse people. I think they can benefit most from coaching and leadership training. Not because they need to improve, but because throughout history in the industrialized world, most leaders and managers have been cisgender males. That means that for the most part, women have not had role models who have looked like them.

Although the numbers seem to be getting better, still only about 29% of top leadership positions in businesses around the world are held by females, and less than 10% of United Nations members have female heads of state (and even fewer gender-diverse leaders). And often, the few highly successful female leaders have a very masculine style. Likely because we learn by watching others.

I know from my own experience, it is hard to find an effective leadership style without depending on masculine behaviors that I have seen work for others. As a woman, it is a great joy to find an authentic feminine leadership style. Having confidence is a critical element to be able to do that. I like to think this book will help many women have the courage to discover and unveil their fully authentic leadership styles.

From the shyest person in the world to the most outgoing person in the world, everyone can benefit from having more confidence. Our level of confidence broadcasts so much information about each of us in every moment of our lives, even if we are unaware of it. When I say confidence, I mean believing in what you are doing, knowing that you are doing the best you can, and not doubting or second-guessing yourself. The goal of this book is to help each individual see her level of confidence clearly, and learn some simple and effective exercises to help increase confidence in all areas of life.

A common issue that comes up in executive coaching sessions, especially (but not only) with my female clients, is confidence. Even the most arrogant person can have a low level of self-confidence. At first impression, they seem like they know everything, but they actually have a lot of doubts, so they project false confidence as a kind of suit of armor. Then there are those of us who are genuinely low in confidence—and show it. These are the people to whom you do not dare point out errors or give feedback, because you think it will genuinely hurt them. You may even fear that these people will break down in tears if you criticize them.

This book focuses on those of you who are somewhere in the middle. You feel confident much of the time, but certain situations or triggers cause you to suddenly feel paralyzed, at a loss for words, with a brain that doesn't seem to function properly.

A word about introversion and extroversion. Broadly speaking, according to Carl Jung, introverts get their energy through reflection and alone time, and may find excessive socialization exhausting. Jung taught us that extroverts get their energy through exchange and interaction, and may find excessive alone time boring or exhausting.

I would like to dispel the myth that extroverts are more confident than introverted people. In my experience, working with thousands of both over the years, I do not see any correlation. It's just that a lack of confidence looks very different in an introvert than in an extrovert. For example, sometimes a low-confidence introvert might become even quieter than usual, and a low-confidence extrovert might become even louder than usual. So, please do your best to let go of stereotypes about yourself and others as you read this book. Each person will find their own version of confidence, no matter where you get your energy.

Margo C. McClimans

STAGES OF CONFIDENCE

Before you read any further, I invite you to reflect on your current level of confidence. How confident do you feel most of the time? "I doubt myself so much that I rarely act on any of my thoughts. I only do things when I am very sure they will work out." Or, "I don't feel the need to prove myself. I am willing to act on most thoughts without worrying about the consequences, and I am genuinely open to feedback about my behaviors, choices and ideas." Or perhaps something in between.

In order to being some structure to your self-reflection, I have identified different stages of confidence. As I explain each one, take mental note of where you spend the most time.

The Cocoon Stage is the characterized by internal focus and self-orientation. Here we have an intense self-consciousness that can sometimes even be perceived as distance or aloofness. In this stage, we have such heavy self-doubt and relentless criticism that we often do not even notice compliments or positive comments at all.

The Dismissal Stage allows us to hear the compliments, but we usually brush them off and consider them bogus. We are slightly less focused on ourselves, so we start to register compliments. However, we cannot bring ourselves to believe them. We reject most positive statements as exaggerations or even as lies.

At the Dependence Stage, we become highly outwardly focused. We seek compliments because they are the fuel for our self-esteem. We do not approve of our own thoughts and actions unless others approve of them too. This is a roller coaster of emotions; we soar when others compliment us, merely coast when people do not acknowledge us, and crash when people criticize us.

The Equanimity Stage is a place of lightness and freedom. Our internal compass is what guides our sense of well-being and confidence, yet we are open to listen to external points of view. We consider that information as data. We learn from it but do not take it personally. We may not always feel great, but we recognize when we are feeling low and know how to get ourselves back into a place of balance.

The Four Channels of Confidence

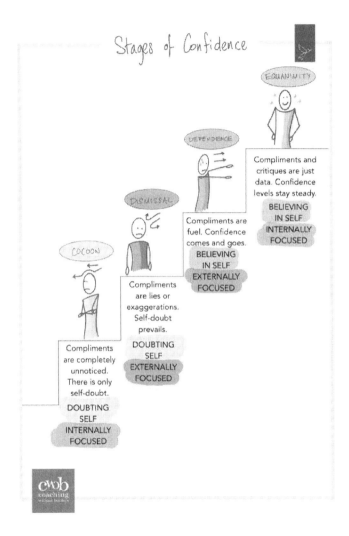

REFLECTION QUESTIONS

Now take a few minutes to digest what you have read and apply it to yourself. Grab a pen and paper, or write directly in this book, and respond to these questions:

What stage of confidence feels most familiar?

What is it like to be in this stage?

How does your stage of confidence shape the way you perceive the world and others in it?

What might be the gift of being at this level of confidence?

What thoughts or emotions do you have, that you feel keep you at this stage?

What will be possible for you when you reach a new stage of confidence?

What level of confidence would you like to have?

As an executive coach, I simply cannot resist asking questions. Your answers will help you understand more about why you are at your current level of confidence. If you haven't already done so, I encourage you to take a few moments right now to write down the thoughts that come to mind as you ponder these questions. No paper handy? There are a few blank pages at the back of this book for you to use. Your answers will stimulate valuable insights and prepare you for our journey together.

WHAT IS CONFIDENCE?

When I say confidence, I don't mean ego. I'm not talking about saying you are the greatest and putting yourself ahead of everybody else. Not at all; that is egotism. Egotism is the feeling or belief that you are better, more important, and more talented than other people.[1] True, deep-running confidence, on the other hand, is quiet. Quiet confidence is being aware of one's capabilities and strengths, but not necessarily drawing attention to them.[2] If you believe in yourself, then you will not feel the need to prove yourself to anybody. Therefore, you will go about your daily business believing in what you are doing, knowing that you are doing the best you can, and not doubting or second-guessing yourself. It gives you fuel to keep moving and keep doing the things that you need to do. It is the self-trust that makes you believe that

---

[1] (Merriam-Webster Online., "egotism")

[2] (Dolaman, Sim, and Wang 2010)

ultimately you will be OK, even if you have a setback.

Another definition of confidence that I really like is, "Confidence is what turns thought into action."[3] People often have good ideas, but they don't take action, because they don't believe in themselves or because they don't believe in their ideas. There is also a concept called "creative confidence."[4] Creativity is not about having more brilliant or better ideas than anybody else; it is actually about just being willing to say your ideas out loud, even if they are potentially wrong. This is the difference between creative people and people who describe themselves as "not creative." It is not that creative people are smarter; it is just that they are more willing to share their ideas. They are more willing to be wrong, so they are more likely to keep coming up with new ideas and pushing their boundaries. Then, after a while, their umpteenth idea turns out to be the golden nugget.

If you don't have the confidence to speak up about your ideas, then you won't even start putting ideas on the table, and so you never get to the golden nugget. This is precisely the confidence I want to help you build. This is the willingness to put thoughts into action without constantly doubting yourself.

I believe that we are born confident. I have never heard of a child who was so filled with self-doubt that she gave up learning how to walk after a few failed attempts. Nope;

---

[3] (Kay and Shipman 2014)

[4] (Kelley and Kelley 2014)

we have no reason not to believe in ourselves as babies. So, if we are not confident now, it is because we have learned to doubt ourselves. We have had experiences that have made it hard to trust ourselves, or to show who we really are to others.

There are four different "channels" of confidence: breath, attitude, voice, and body. These four channels broadcast your level of confidence, whether you realize it or not. In other words, you can pick up on cues to determine whether someone is feeling confident or not, by studying her breathing, attitude, voice, and body. We send signals via these four channels that transmit our level of confidence to the people around us. But it is not just about broadcasting confidence to the outside. It is about feeling confident on the inside, for your own sake. It is possible to "tune in" to these four channels, to work on and raise your own genuine level of confidence from the inside. As you learn to adjust your frequency in these four channels, you will immediately feel an impact in your level of confidence. At first, it requires focus and attention, but the more you do the exercises I am about to explain, the more natural it becomes. Soon it will be second nature to feel confident in all four channels.

Margo C. McClimans

1. THE BREATH CHANNEL

We have all listened to presentations in which speakers seem breathless. They almost can't get the words out, and they sound like their mouths have gone dry. It is painful to witness, because we know that horrible feeling ourselves! We have all been there at one point or another, whether we have made a presentation to clients, or stood up before our colleagues in a meeting room. We hope the people listening don't notice, but we just cannot seem to multitask breathing and talking anymore! That being said, it is important to be aware of your breath not just when you are on stage.

With every passing day, we are learning more about the dramatic impact the quality of your breathing has on your health and well-being. We can survive without food for months, without sleep for weeks, and without water for days. But without breathing, we can survive for only a matter of minutes. Breathing is, hands down, the most essential element to life. Yet, we neglect our breathing and take it for granted. Most of us go for days and days without ever being aware of breathing in and breathing out at all. Now, as you are reading this, I bet your breathing has already gotten deeper. The simple act of awareness is all you need to increase the quality of your breathing. How do you feel compared to a few minutes ago?

It is very hard to feel confident when we are tired, stressed or depressed. Although it is not a complete solution to these ailments, breathing deeper, slower, and through your nose has a significant positive effect on energy levels, resilience to stress and mood. And the best thing? Breathing is a tool that is always available, free of charge, and built in, so you can never forget it at home!

Your breathing is a visible sign of your level of confidence. It is also a channel that can allow you to feel and exude a high level of confidence, if you work on it.

Of all the channels of confidence, breathing is the most important, because it supports the other three channels. Deep breathing reduces the levels of the stress hormone cortisol in your blood, allowing your full brain to work well. Now, take a moment to shift your body posture in a way that will help you take a deep breath. What did you do? Likely, you sat up straighter, you may have also put your shoulders back, and uncrossed your arms and legs. All of these put your body in a strong, open position, which also promotes confidence. Breathing also helps you tame your inner critic and have a more confident attitude. Moreover, as every singer knows, your voice is much stronger when you have full lungs.

We breathe all the time, so what is the big deal?

Many people breathe incorrectly and they don't even know it.

Typically, people breathe in a shallow manner from their chest; their chest rises only slightly when they breathe in, and falls when they breathe out. That kind of breathing helps us survive, but if we want to thrive, we should be breathing deeply from our abdomens.

You can think of your lungs as balloons; they do not actually have any muscles in them. Lungs expand and contract because of the muscle underneath them, called the diaphragm. The diaphragm moves up into the chest cavity like a plate being raised directly upward, pushing the air out of the lungs. At the end of the exhalation, the diaphragm automatically moves down into the abdomen to create more space for the lungs, which pulls in more air as you breathe in. If you breathe fully, letting the diaphragm go down into your abdomen as far as possible, your stomach will stick out a bit when you have a full, deep breath in your body. Therefore, if you are breathing fully, then you will feel your stomach move out, and your chest will not move much. Your chest and shoulders can be still, but your stomach should stick out when you have taken in a full, deep breath. As you exhale fully, your stomach goes in.

By the way, what have we women (and men) been taught to do with our stomachs? Hold them in, right? Especially on stage or at the front of a room when everyone is watching us! No wonder it is so hard to feel calm and grounded when we are giving a speech, or presenting in front of colleagues and clients. We can't breathe properly if we hold our bellies in all the time!

It is good practice to do some exaggerated breaths, just to see how deeply you can actually breathe, and compare that to how you normally breathe.

Step 1: **Inflate the "balloon."** Start to inhale slowly through your nose, filling up your lungs and imagining that your stomach is a balloon you are inflating. Try putting your hand on your stomach, so you can feel it beginning to protrude as you breathe in.

Step 2: **Open the "auxiliary cavity."** When you feel like the bottom part of your lungs is full (your balloon is fully inflated), then continue to inhale by slowly lifting your chest to create even more space for your lungs. Imagine a string attached to the center of your sternum, being pulled directly up toward the ceiling until you cannot inhale anymore.

Step 3: **Let the air out.** Part your lips slightly, and control the speed of your exhale by keeping your mouth almost closed. Let the air escape through the small hole in your lips, slowly and evenly. Feel your stomach deflate, and at the very end of the breath, you can even bend forward slightly to help let out the old, stale air.

In choir practice, we used to do breathing exercises like this to learn how to hold a note longer. On the exhalation, we would sing a note and see who could hold the note the longest. Timing yourself this way can be a fun method of practicing your deep-breathing ability. See how long you can make your exhalation last. I have counted my own as long as 36 seconds, but I am sure many of you could make yours even longer.

Now that you are breathing properly, I will take you through a few specific breathing techniques that are useful in particular situations.

COOLING BREATH

The first one is called the cooling breath.[5] This is the kind of breath to use when you start to feel very angry. Think of the kind of situation where you think you might explode, or break out in tears, or have to leave the room because you're so upset. Interestingly, this breath is also useful if other people in the room are angry, or showing a lot of emotion. Emotions are contagious, and the cooling breath will help you avoid being impacted by another person's anger.

The cooling breath is done by breathing in through

---

[5] (Melnick 2013)

your mouth and out through your nose. As you breathe in through your mouth, you just allow a tiny little hole between your lips, and let the air pass over your tongue as you breathe in. Hold your mouth as if you're drinking through a straw. If you're doing this correctly, the air will feel cool.

Lots of times when I introduce this to a live audience, people say, "Oh, I can't do that when I'm in the middle of a meeting. I'll look ridiculous!" But you don't have to exaggerate, and appear that you're breathing through a straw. You can do this in a very subtle way. Try it now.

Anyway, if there's a big meeting going on, especially if there are angry people around, no one is going to notice that I'm holding my mouth like I have a straw in it. However, it can help me calm down. It can help me soothe my nerves. And as we said, emotions are contagious. So if I'm calmer, I can hopefully have a calming impact on the people around me as well.

RAPID CLEARING BREATH

Our bodies produce cortisol when the brain thinks it is going to need a big metabolic output. This is often the case when we face stressful situations. Although cortisol is a very helpful hormone (it is what we need to get our blood pumping enough to get out of bed in the morning), when kept at high levels regularly and for extended periods, it impacts our physical well-being in many ways, most of them negative. Although sometimes disputed, research has shown that when cortisol pumps through our veins, we feel less confident.[6] I talk a lot more about this in the Body Channel chapter.

One way to get rid of excess cortisol from our bloodstreams, is to take deep breaths.[7] In her book, Success Under Stress, Sharon Melnick talks about a certain breath that you can take to reduce the amount of cortisol in your blood. She calls it the "rapid clearing breath." It's not called rapid because you breathe in and out quickly. It's about rapidly clearing out the hormones in your blood that make you feel stressed out and nervous. It's a rapid way of relaxing.

It entails breathing in through your nose for three counts, and breathing out through your mouth for six. Some people may prefer to breathe in for four and out for eight; you decide exactly how many counts you want to do. The important thing is that you breathe in for half as long as you breathe out, and therefore get out all the old, stale carbon dioxide and take in fresh air.

You breathe in relatively deeply for three counts, and the exhalation is double as long to rid your body of stress. If you do this for three minutes and if you could test your blood before and after, you would see a lower amount of cortisol in your blood. You will feel more confident.

---

[6] (Carney, Cuddy, and Yap 2010)
[7] (Melnick 2013)

It is incredible what a difference a few minutes of controlled breathing can make when it comes to increasing your confidence. Learn how to breathe properly, and then practice this daily.

SILENCE

Get over the fear of the momentary silence that will happen as you take a breath, which can be especially difficult when we are presenting. When we give a speech or presentation, for some reason, we have a completely distorted picture of how long silences are. We think that if silence lasts for more than a second or two, people will think we have forgotten something or somehow will find us unprepared. On the contrary! Silence is one of the best tools we have when making a presentation, for three simple reasons.

1. **Silence is an underappreciated attention-getter.** Unfortunately, if we do not vary our voice enough, people stop listening; it becomes just sound to them. When we pause in our speech and allow a few seconds of silence, it creates a break in the sound and people look up to see what is happening.

2. **People need time to ponder and respond.** As a matter of practice, whenever I put a question to my audience, I always allow seven seconds of silence for them to answer. This feels like an absolute eternity when you are on stage. However, this is when people who are not

normally the first ones to speak, get a chance to chime in and contribute, often bringing some of the most valuable insights to the group.

3. **You get a chance to breathe!** Once you get used to allowing and building in pauses and silence in your presentations, you can use those breaks as time to breathe properly. This gives you a chance to get your nerves under control, metabolize any excess cortisol in your system, and stay as confident as possible.

At the beginning of my career, I used to write on top of my presentation note cards in huge letters: SLOW… PAUSE… BREATHE! This reminded me to take a breath. It seems obvious, but sometimes we literally just forget to breathe properly. A little reminder can make all the difference.

PHYSIOLOGICAL SIGH[8]

This breath is an even faster way to tell your brain that it is OK to engage the parasympathetic nervous system. It involves taking a deep breath in, filling your lungs fully, then forcing in one last extra "sip" of air, just when you thought you couldn't inhale anymore. Then, exhaling completely, until you have empty lungs.

This last little push of air forces open the alveoli that

---

[8] Developed by Dr. Andrew D. Huberman of Stanford School of Medicine
https://scopeblog.stanford.edu/2020/10/07/how-stress-affects-your-brain-and-how-to-reverse-it

sometimes stay closed when we are breathing normally. It adds an additional push of oxygen, decreasing the level of carbon dioxide in your bloodstream. When we have increased carbon dioxide in the blood, it signals a stress response. The physiological sigh reverses that. It is great practice to do the physiological sigh regularly to combat longer-term stress, but it can also be extremely helpful in critical moments of tension or anxiety.

I recently taught this to my 12-year-old step-daughter, while waiting in line for a roller coaster at an amusement park. She wanted to go on the ride, but began to get uncomfortably nervous as we approached the front of the line. I helped her take a few physiological sighs, and she reported her heart rate calmed down and she was ready to fully enjoy the ride.

REFLECTION QUESTIONS

What is the quality of my breathing right now?

How can I remind myself to breathe more deeply at all times?

Which breathing technique do I want to experiment with this week?

2. THE ATTITUDE CHANNEL

The Attitude Channel has to do with our interior world. It's what we tell ourselves on the inside, that then shows up on the outside.

Have you ever met a woman who just seems confident? She walks into a room, and you instinctively know she is not worried about what other people may think. It is not that she doesn't care what other people think; she is simply not worried about their opinions. Any group will contain some people who look confident and some people who do not look confident. You can just tell. The ones who have a confident attitude are the ones who seem to be reasonably comfortable around new people or circumstances. The key element of having a confident attitude is how you deal with your own saboteur.

I first learned about the concept of the saboteur when I was getting my coaching certification, with the Coaches

Training Institute[9] back in 2005. It was life-changing for me, as I realized how many inner critic voices I had, shaping the way I thought about myself.

Everyone in the world has a saboteur voice.[10] These are our inner critics. I believe that women suffer from them more than men, and that the saboteur impacts women's choices more than men let it impact their choices. Of course, men are not immune. I have helped hundreds of male managers learn to identify and pacify their saboteurs, so they can achieve more.

In new or uncomfortable situations, a confident person just does something even if she doesn't know what she is supposed to do. A woman who has a confident attitude has a confident mindset. An unconscious part of her brain that believes she deserves a seat at the table and her voice to be heard. As I said at the start of this book, I believe we are all born with this mindset. The work is to go back and uncover that part of you.

This confident mindset is often subconscious. But if it were conscious, it might say something like, "I don't know what I'm supposed to be doing, but I'm not worried about getting it wrong. I will just do my best to manage this situation and see how it goes."

That kind of mindset or set of beliefs is what is possible when we are able to let go of the saboteur voice.

---

[9] https://coactive.com
[10] (Whitworth, Kimsey-House, Kimsey-House, and Sandahl 1998)

On the other side of the coin, the women who do not seem confident, may not have a confident attitude. They are the ones who don't initiate things; they wait until someone speaks to them rather than walking up to people and reaching out to shake their hand. These women often have a dominant saboteur voice inside (even if they are not aware of it), telling them to hold back.

Saboteur comes from the French word sabotage, which is derived from the word sabot, a heavy wooden shoe worn by factory workers. In the early 20th century, unhappy workers would throw their sabots into the wooden gears of the textile looms to break the cogs, because they feared that automated machines would render the human workers obsolete.[11] They sabotaged the machines with their sabots. Therefore, the workers' fear of change and their deep fear of becoming obsolete caused them to destroy the path to change. That is exactly what our inner saboteur does to us.

Our saboteur wants to keep the status quo, because whatever we are doing now has not killed us, so it must be safe. It "protects" us by stopping us in our tracks whenever we want to step out, do something new, try something risky, grow, or develop a new behavior. A saboteur can be an incredibly strong force, provoking fear and anxiety in us that can be debilitating. Don't get me wrong: the saboteur is not evil. It is just our own ego trying to protect us from any potential pain or

---

[11] (Hodson and Sullivan 1995, 69)

embarrassment. At the same time though, it "protects" us from growth and discovering our full potential.

For example, imagine an office party at your new place of work. It happens to be your first day and you know no one. You realize this is your chance to meet people and feel more at home in your new office environment. As you stand alone and survey the room, you see various groups of people happily chatting to one another. Your saboteur says, "Those people don't want to talk to you, it's going to be awkward," or "They are enjoying talking to each other, and you would be a disruption," or "You would seem overly eager if you introduce yourself; you would look silly."

Does this inner dialogue sound familiar?

When you do not have a confident attitude, you heed the saboteur's warnings (usually without even realizing there was a saboteur at all) and stay glued to the spot, maybe pulling out your cell phone and having a look, grabbing a snack or downing a drink or two.

Every woman's saboteur says something slightly different to her, yet the theme is often the same: "You are not good enough." Having coached and trained thousands of managers since 2005, I have come to the conclusion that everyone has this voice, from the most confident to the meekest; it is just that not everyone listens to it all the time. As you begin to be conscious of and learn to manage your saboteur voice, new possibilities open up to you.

So, in the same workplace scenario, when you have a confident attitude, you brush aside the saboteur's commentary, casually walk up to a new group, and make eye contact with the person speaking, and smile. (Notice: you do not break into the conversation like a bull in a china shop.) You quietly make a connection with the new people, and join the conversation when someone says hello or asks you a question. Have you ever noticed that it is very hard to ignore a person who is making eye contact with you and smiling?

A big difference between these two people, is their ability to be in the here and now. The saboteur constantly pulls you out of the present moment, to focus you on past failings or anxiety about future consequences. Like the Wizard of Oz's Wicked Witch of the West, who melts away when she gets wet, your saboteur voice melts away as you bring your focus back to the present moment.

For those of us who find ourselves somewhere in between those two attitudes, the power comes in sharpening our skill of noticing. First, we have to notice that the saboteur is talking, which is no small task. Most of us have already been unconsciously obeying our saboteur for decades. When we bring ourselves back to the present, then we can choose to either ignore the saboteur, or consciously say to ourselves, "It's OK, I could do this, but I'm not up for it today." That conscious choice is the key to start developing a confident attitude.

The strength of your confident attitude depends on

how well you manage your saboteur. And this requires self-awareness. Often, the saboteur builds on things that we've heard in childhood—critiques from parents and teachers, or teasing from classmates and siblings. The things we hear about ourselves growing up, help define how we perceive ourselves. Our saboteur voice picks up on the negative memories and uses them as potent fuel to prevent us from doing new things, to keep us feeling "safe" by confirming and perpetuating our beliefs about ourselves and the world.

What if my saboteur is right?

I talk about saboteurs a lot with my clients, and sometimes they are skeptical. They say things like, "Well, my saboteur is right! I have to listen to it; it's not just crazy talk. That stuff is true!" Some of what our saboteurs say to us is based on truth, and that's part of the reason why what it says is so attractive. It's so believable because it picks up on your real fears, many of which are based on past experiences. There is bias in the world. The saboteur is right that the world has risks. The question is: Do you want to stay safe, or live up to your full potential?

Even if you are convinced that your saboteur tells you the truth sometimes, you always have a choice whether or not you want to listen to it. And even if you still "obey" your saboteur voice 90% of the time, that is OK. You will be amazed at what a difference that 10% will make in your confidence levels over the long run.

THE GOOD-GIRL SABOTEUR

My personal saboteur voice tells me many things, but the main one is:

"You should be a good girl."

Which has multiplied itself to suit most any circumstance by morphing into:

"You should be a good daughter."

"You should be a good mother."

"You should be a good friend."

"You should be a good sister."

"You should be a good citizen."

Not that those aren't valiant goals. But when they step on my own sense of autonomy and prevent me from doing what is actually best for my health and well-being, they become limiting. In these cases, the saboteur goes on to say, "Don't say something or do something that will make people not like you. You need to be accepted to be worthy." Even though nowadays I am much better at noticing and pushing aside my saboteur voice, when I am not aware of it, I am generally driven to always be nice and polite, even if someone makes me angry. It tells me that I am not good enough or don't deserve what I want, so I should not speak up or ask for it. (This is usually bundled with feelings of guilt for not being grateful for what I have.)

My good-girl saboteur comes into play by telling me, "You are going to create an inconvenience for other people." An example is one morning in the car. I was driving home from the tennis courts, and came to an intersection that has no markings. In Switzerland, that means that whoever is on the right has the right of way. I had the right of way, but I saw this giant courier van pulling up fast, so I stopped and he abruptly halted. I proceeded, and he turned onto the same road behind me. This also happened to be a 30km/h (20mph) zone. I assumed that because he was a delivery person, he must know these roads well and must be in a hurry, and he probably wanted to zip around me so he could do his job. I noticed myself checking to see if he was following me closely, because I felt I didn't want to get in his way, as he was in a hurry. Automatically my saboteur told me, "That guy is more important than me; I should be a 'good girl' and let him go around me."

CONFIDENCE AND NOTICING

YOUR SABOTEUR

Then I thought, "No." I took note of my saboteur and said to myself, "No, I am actually going to drive at the speed limit, because that's what I am comfortable with, and if he is impatient, that is his problem."

If I had not acknowledged my saboteur, and instead let it take over, I might have gone faster than the speed limit just to make life easier for the delivery person, assuming he wanted to go fast. The consequences might have been that I would have driven dangerously or received a speeding ticket.

See how the saboteur is actually self-sabotage? The saboteur pretended to keep me "safe" by making me look like a good little girl in the eyes of the courier, so that he wouldn't be annoyed with me. Our saboteurs are not rational.

Learning to recognize your saboteur is a critical first step to strengthening the Attitude Channel.

THE NOT-QUALIFIED/EXPERIENCED-ENOUGH SABOTEUR

Saboteurs like to remind us just before critical moments: "OK, don't forget, you better not do something that makes you look stupid—better not to do anything at all." Or, "Don't speak up unless you are 100% sure of what you are going to say." What the saboteur really means is, "I want to keep you safe; I want to keep your ego protected."

Another of my saboteurs tells me, "I'm not experienced enough." My whole life, I always found myself with older people—older friends, older classmates, older colleagues. This came to pass again when I first started working as a coach. I was hired as an external coach by a large multinational corporation for the first time. Up until then, I had been doing coaching and leadership development with MBA students. My first program consisted of three fellow coaches, 24 participants, and myself. The participants were managers for this organization, who had flown in from multiple countries to attend this elite leadership program.

My saboteur was in overdrive, because I was the youngest of my colleagues by at least ten years. If I had been looking at it from a neutral standpoint, I would have seen a group of four coaches that had a nice variety: men and women, different ages, different nationalities. But no, my saboteur wanted to emphasize that I was too young and too inexperienced, and therefore I didn't deserve to be there. It was my first time doing that kind of program. Part of the work entailed presenting concepts to and running exercises with all 24 participants. In addition, my fellow (highly experienced) coaches were of course there, listening as well.

It was my turn in front of the room. It was a simple task; I had to run an introduction round. It was a one-minute challenge, so part of my job was to make sure people stayed within the minute, and I had to cut them off if they went longer. I went through the 24 participants without any issues. But then I got to my colleagues. One colleague went over the minute, and I jumped in and said,

"Actually, that is over a minute." I kind of made a joke about it, but I did stop him, so he wrapped it up and didn't say anything else at the time. Immediately afterwards, while moving out into the hallway to go to the next session, he came up to me and said my reaction was "not OK." After I asked what was not OK for him, he replied, "You have to let me talk more because I am one of the coaches," and added something about his credibility being impacted.

At this point, my saboteur was totally fueled, saying to me, "See, you don't have enough experience. You should have known that." As if I should magically know things! Even though it was a small mistake, in the next session, I felt so much worse about myself, and I started doubting every little choice that I had to make. It was difficult to stay present. That is exactly the plague of the saboteur. If we are not aware of it, it knocks down our confidence levels even more. Consequently, I was at risk of letting my now-rattled nerves sabotage me the next time I presented.

CONFIDENCE AND YOUR PERSONAL MANTRA

Thankfully, I was able to get back on track, with the technique of using a mantra.

A mantra is a statement that people repeat frequently. People originally started using mantras as part of meditation to aid in concentration.[12] I could feel that I was

---

[12] (Merriam-Webster Online, "mantra")

nervous, and I combated that nervousness by building and then maintaining a more confident attitude.

I said to myself, "Alright, I may not have as much experience as my colleagues, but I am a certified coach, and I have received lots of positive feedback about my coaching." I found a small but secure source of genuine confidence. I latched onto that area of confidence, and held on even when I felt less confident about other areas.

I had been working with a coach myself over the previous year, and he had helped me discover a way of getting my energy back and feeling grounded. We had identified a very short exercise to do this. I just had to go somewhere I could see the sky and take a few deep breaths. So I went over to the window, took a few deep breaths (which always recharges me), and said to myself, "You know what? Even though I may be the youngest here, who knows? I may be the best coach that my participants have had." There was no way I could prove that sentence; however, there was a small chance that it might be true. Just that little, but real, possibility was enough to make me feel better. It had nothing to do with comparing myself to the other coaches. It wouldn't have mattered which other coaches were present, I had a mantra that helped me. My mantra was something for me to hang on to. Suddenly, I could feel I was more confident. I was more comfortable if I made a mistake or if I stepped on somebody's toes here and there, because I felt the possibility that I may have been the best coach the participants had ever had. My little mantra "I may be the best coach they have had" was the perfect antidote for my "You're not experienced enough" saboteur.

A close cousin of this saboteur is the "not-qualified-enough" saboteur, which shows up for assessments or around the time of a job interview.

When you apply for a job, of course you look at the requirements and skills needed. It is very difficult for everybody to meet 100% of those requirements. Internal research by Hewlett-Packard found that women apply only for jobs for which they feel they are a 100% match; men, however, apply even when they meet no more than 60% of the requirements.[13] If that has been you and you don't apply, you may have a saboteur voice saying things like, "You're not good enough. They are not going to want you. You don't have enough experience. You haven't studied enough." Those are just assumptions that keep you "safe" from the potential difficulties you might face if you applied.

The saboteur simply wants the status quo, even though it might mean missing out on a new and exciting job for you. It is a new step, and it's outside your comfort zone; therefore, the saboteur holds you back. The man who meets only 60% of requirements and applies anyway, apparently does not hear the saboteur, or he is able to ignore it. Therefore, he is able to say, "Well, I meet

---

[13] (The Economist, The Feminist Mystique 2013)

most of the requirements. It's worth a try; let's just go for it." This is confidence; he is doing something even if he has doubt.

THE NOT-ATTRACTIVE-ENOUGH SABOTEUR

Another saboteur that plagues and distracts women is "You are not attractive enough." Mine likes to tell me that I'm fat, which is something I got teased about when I was a little girl. I was always the friend and never the girlfriend through school years. Even though I have managed to reach and maintain a normal weight in my adult years, my saboteur still likes to rip me away from the here and now, and blind me to my normal BMI body, to remind me of the past. No matter what the scale says, I need to be constantly vigilant to ignore that saboteur voice and remind myself that my weight is actually just fine now. And, yes, just maybe, I am even attractive.

During my single years, even though I was a healthy weight and physically fit, one of my saboteur's favorite times to speak up was when I was near an attractive man. It would repeat, "You're not skinny enough and you're not pretty enough to get that guy." It would say, "You better lean on showing you are smart and funny."

Luckily, I learned to give myself a choice as to whether or not I would listen to that voice. That was possible because I was aware of it. I would acknowledge the presence of the saboteur, take a few deep breaths, push the critical voice away, and then make some steamy eye contact with the guy across the room. It was amazing how well that worked.

Later in life, going through pregnancy and watching the numbers on the scale rise week by week, I had a new battle with my saboteur. I felt much of the progress I had made in tackling my "You're fat" saboteur was lost. I was overly upset when my weight gain on certain weeks was above the normal curve.

It was a reminder that the work of maintaining confidence is a lifelong practice, not a "check the box and get it done" exercise. I gained 14kg over the course of my pregnancy, and took one year to return to my previous weight. I had problems with breast feeding, and was pained to hear that breast feeding is what helps mothers lose weight after pregnancy. I struggled with feelings not only of being unattractive, but also that I was not maternal enough, or that I was doing breast feeding "wrong". Suddenly my saboteur had a whole new category of "not good enough" to work with. Moreover, I was back to work running my own business and experiencing the guilt of not being home with my precious new son enough. I was burning the candle at both ends and perceived myself as falling short in every arena.

I was upset not only by the new challenges that I did not know how to overcome, but also by the fact that I "should" know how to stay confident. After all, I had written a book about it! My saboteur was having a heyday.

CONFIDENCE AND SELF-CARE

How did I get back on track? I started prioritizing self-care. One fine day, when my son was about two or three months old, I somehow managed to take some extra time for myself after a shower. I took time to cream up every inch of my body. After I cut my toenails, I took time to trim away all the excess cuticles. I plucked my eyebrows thoroughly, and massaged oil into my fingernails. These were things that I had not managed to do for months. All of a sudden, I became aware that I was feeling calm, more calm than I had felt in a long time. And I felt more confident. I had a clear head and felt able to focus on what a wonderful life I had. My saboteur is loudest when I am under stress, have not had enough sleep, and have little or no time for myself.

I had a conversation with my partner Lukas; we agreed to take turns being "in charge." No longer would we just wait and see who was going to react to the next cry or need for a diaper change. It would be the person in charge who did that. We even put it in our shared calendar, so we knew for sure who was in change and that it was evenly balanced. This meant, for example, that suddenly I had my Saturday mornings free. Without needing to ask or double-check with Lukas, I could go to my exercise class, get a manicure, meet friends for coffee or get some extra work done if I wanted to. This time for myself was essential to get my confidence back. My saboteur no longer berated me every time I was away from my son, because I knew he was well cared for, and I would have plenty of time with him when it was my turn to be in charge later that day. Lukas had agreed to be in charge, and I was free to look after my own needs. This, of course, was true for Lukas, too. Which helped him feel better about taking time for himself too. We also made sure to plan for date nights, one-on-one days with the older kids, and family time, to make sure each constellation of our family relationships was getting attention.

Now when my confidence slips and my inner critic gets active, I know to stop and take care of myself. I put reminders in my calendar to book massages and facials for myself regularly. I have a Happy Healthy Margo morning and evening routine in my daily checklist. They include things like stretching, meditating, use face roller, floss, nail oil, pluck eyebrows, write three wins that I had that day in my journal, and walking my son to school in the morning. I don't always complete all of them, but I find it helpful to remind myself regularly that these things help me maintain my health, happiness, and therefore confidence.

Once you have a confident attitude, it will be much easier to recognize the saboteur and ignore it. Or, just say to yourself, "No, I don't care. It's not true. I know that's just an old fear of mine. I'm going to do what I desire to do anyway."

We will probably never get rid of the saboteur voices entirely. However, we can manage them. The key is to become good at recognizing them. That ability gives us power, because we then have a choice. If we are able to distinguish our saboteur voices from our true desires, then we will discover the magic antidote. The moment we recognize the saboteur, we can bring ourselves back to the present moment and say, "OK, my saboteur tells me I am not good enough. Is that true, or is that something I want to ignore?" And then we have a choice—the power to turn thoughts into actions. The second we feel that we don't have a choice, we feel like victims. When we are in "victim mode" we are completely powerless.

My recommendation is not to try to eliminate or kill your saboteur, but instead, learn how to notice it. Get to know it like a lifelong companion, so that you can have the choice at all times whether or not to follow it. Maybe even befriend it. After all, that cute little saboteur is only trying to protect you. Making peace with your saboteur will dissolve its hold on you.

How do you know if your saboteur voice is speaking?

A couple of signs show clearly that the saboteur is around.

1. **You feel guilty.** Take the example of the courier driver; I felt guilty for driving in front of him and slowing him down. That was the saboteur.

2. **You say, "I should" (instead of "I need to" or "I want to").** If you really think that you need to do something, you will say, "I need to get out of his way" or

"I want to get out of his way," not "I should get out of his way." "Need" and "want" are completely different than "should." "Should" shows that you are doubting yourself, rather than believing in yourself and being confident.

3. **You are thinking about past mistakes or worried about future consequences.** The saboteur pokes a hole in your confidence by taunting you with negative possibilities.

I would like to share some tools to help you lead a fulfilling life and become more confident, without letting the saboteur make your decisions for you.

TOOLS FOR PACIFYING THE SABOTEUR VOICE

I use the term pacifying quite deliberately. And our goal is not to destroy our saboteur, it is to accept it, befriend it and learn to let it serve us rather than hinder us. We use pacifiers to help calm babies. Your saboteur voice can be thought of as the crying baby in your mind that is scared or uncomfortable and wants attention. Your saboteur is not the enemy. It is part of you. And just as it is important to treat yourself with kindness and compassion, a gentle approach is most effective with your saboteur.

Notice your saboteur. The key to building confidence, is to learn about yourself and learn about your saboteur. This way, you can be prepared to respond to challenging situations rationally, rather than giving in to a saboteur-fueled, knee-jerk reaction. Take a few moments and answer the below questions about yourself. Once you have done so, you will be able to recognize the saboteur when it is there, and actively choose to ignore it.

What kinds of people or situations trigger a dip in self-confidence in you?

What is your Achilles' heel[14] and what does your saboteur tell you about it?

What does your saboteur say, and when? Fill in the blanks:

   i. "You are too_____"

   ii. "You are not_____enough"

   iii. "I am always_____"

   iv. "I never_____"

Develop a personal mantra. A mantra is a statement about yourself that you can repeat to yourself over and over in a moment of self-doubt. A personal mantra:

is based on a strength of yours

is specific and situational

contains the word "might"

---

[14] An Achilles' heel is a fault or weakness that causes or could cause someone or something to fail (Merriam-Webster Online, "Achilles' heel").

is not provable

might be true, even if it is just a 1% chance

if true, would make you feel really confident!

Although affirmations e.g., "You are worthy" are powerful, they are different than a personal mantra. They can feel too unrealistic to be useful in a moment of self-doubt. Mantras are also not lying to yourself, e.g., "You are a superstar!" A mantra really might be true, and instantly makes you feel different about yourself when you imagine the possibility that it is really true; e.g., before a meeting, you may say, "My ideas might make all the difference." Or before a big presentation, "I might really rock this."

Self-care. Actions speak louder than words. When we love something, we look after it. When we look after something, it flourishes. When we neglect something, it is a sign that our priorities are elsewhere. The same is true of taking care of yourself. And if self-neglect persists, eventually we have no more energy to look after anything. Nothing tells your inner critic that you are worthy like some good old-fashioned self-care, whatever that means for you. When we are confident, our subconscious mind is less occupied with ourselves and self-criticism, so we are also more able to give attention to others. It's like the oxygen mask in the airplane: you need to put your own mask on first, so that you are able to help others.

Listen to your emotions. What does your gut tell you? What does your heart tell you? Ask yourself, "What do I really want?" Your emotions are data, they are a way for your wisdom to send you information. And emotions don't lie. Every emotion has a purpose, e.g., anger tells you something needs to change, frustration is a signal that you need help. Happiness is a sign that what is happening should be preserved, rewarded or reinforced. We often push aside or suppress our emotions, especially in the workplace, to avoid feeling uncomfortable or for fear of being labeled "emotional". However, our emotions are a great source of wisdom and a counterbalance to our saboteur voice. It is not always easy to pay attention to your emotions though, especially after years learning to ignore them. One way to quiet your inner critic voice and hear what your gut or emotions have to tell you, is the Fast Shift Method:[15]

Soften your eyes and de-focus your gaze, and tune into the space between your eyes and the objects in front of you.

Soft eyes: relax your eyes and all the muscles around them, while keeping them open.

Next, allow your tongue to be soft and relaxed.

Mouth open slightly. Soft eyes. Soft tongue.

Now have a focus on your belly. Breathe into your belly and soften it.

---

[15] Developed by Dr. Mark Atkinson, MBBS, BSc and learned from Felix Hirschburger, MA

If possible, hold an inner smile.

Without returning to the front of the head to think, be with your soft tongue. You will notice the mind has gone quiet.

Now close your eyes, and count down backwards, 5, 4, 3, 2, 1, while breathing into and softening your lower belly. As you count down, tilt your head down and scan your attention slowly down your body to your stomach area. Relax. Do nothing. Listen. See if any feelings, words or messages arise. If you have followed the above method exactly, this is very likely your wisdom speaking, not your saboteur.

5. **Replace "should" with "could".** If you find yourself using should in a sentence, practice replacing it with could. "I should really call her" becomes "I could call her." Suddenly, you have a choice! You could call her. Choice is empowering, and that brings a feeling of confidence.

6. **Mindfulness.** Your saboteur thrives on memories and predictions. It foretells disaster and negative outcomes, and regurgitates past mistakes and embarrassments. The saboteur burns with worries and regrets, and is extinguished when deprived of thoughts of past and future. The more you are able to gently guide your mind to focus on the present moment, the faster your saboteur voice will fade away.

7. **End-of-day audit.** When you are first learning to

recognize your saboteur, this exercise is especially helpful. At the end of your day, when you are lying down to sleep, do an audit of your day. Think through your whole day and recall how many times your saboteur voice impacted your decisions or your behaviors. Do this every night for a week. You will probably be able to start drawing a pattern and understanding any recurring themes. This exercise is easier than trying to notice your saboteur in real time, and it builds your ability to catch your saboteur in action in the future.

Experiment with these tools and techniques, and find out which ones feel good to you and give the best results.

What I have noticed is that at first, they can be somewhat difficult, yet it soon becomes second nature to use them. It requires focus and energy in the beginning. You may get off track or forget to practice these things. But don't let that fuel your saboteur, hang in there!

CONFIDENCE AND JUDGMENT

Do you talk about other people in a negative way? For example, how stupid this or that person looked or sounded. Or what a hideous dress so and so was wearing. Having a laugh at others' expense may give you short-term satisfaction or fun. But in the long run, it will have the opposite effect. Gossiping, judging and/or bad-mouthing others sharpens your brain's ability to judge, which will inevitably be used by your saboteur against you later.

If you judge others, you are generally training your brain to be critical, negative and judgmental. This will only reinforce your ability to be cruel to yourself, too. Moreover judgment is often preceded by comparison. I believe there is no faster recipe for unhappiness than comparing ourselves to others. One of my favorite quotes is "Comparison is the thief of joy" attributed to Teddy Roosevelt.

So why do we do it? Judgment is a mechanism we use to bring a sense of certainty to an uncertain world. None of us actually knows what is going to happen, and the less comfortable we are with that reality, the more we try to control outcomes. We judge things as right or wrong, good or bad, and then proceed accordingly. It provides a (oftentimes false) sense of order and control.

And if you are in this very moment judging what I am saying as correct or incorrect, I will ask you to refrain from passing judgment, and instead engage your curiosity. How do you do that? Pause and ask yourself, "I wonder where this is going? I wonder how my mindset might be expanded by being open to this perspective?" Question rather than assume you already know.

It is natural to judge, it is yet another form of our saboteur "protecting" us from the new, the unknown and the uncertain. We judge all the time without realizing it.

Judgment prevents us from being open to new experiences, new perspectives, and it creates disconnection from the people around us. Again, self-awareness is key if we want to stay open to learn, grow and connect with others.

The people around us who are the most judgmental, tend to be highly critical of themselves, too. So, it helps to approach them with compassion. Instead of ignoring, or worse, supporting, their judgmental comments about others, provide a different perspective. We hope our friends don't judge us, but first we need to look in the mirror and make sure we are not judging.

I will always remember the moment I realized I was judgmental. In my mid-twenties. Up until that point, I thought of myself as a non-judgmental person. It still stings to admit this. I was in a restaurant with my ex-boyfriend's mother; let's call her Maria. A woman walked by with a very revealing dress. Something in me (my own insecurity!) felt the need to express my disapproval about this woman's outfit. I think I wanted Maria to think of me as a wholesome girl. I wanted her to like me. So, I made a disapproving comment and Maria looked at the woman, then turned to me and said, "She has a nice body, she looks great." I was flabbergasted! And schooled! She showed such grace and benevolence, I learned from her that day not only how to be non-judgmental, but also how to kindly redirect someone else's judgment.

I like to think I have come a long way since then, and

most of the work has actually been about learning to manage my inner critic, and not to judge myself. This is an on-going battle though!

Judgment often takes the form of gossip. Gossip is toxic, even if the information being gossiped about is true, because it is shared with negative intent. Even though many people gossip about others as a way to deal with their own insecurities, hoping others will look worse than they do, ironically gossiping can actually make you even more insecure. Gossiping about others erodes your self-confidence, because you never know when people will overhear you, or find out that you have been speaking badly of them. Just like lying, this puts a weight on your subconscious mind, because you must keep track of what you said to whom, and be ready to deal with it, if it ever comes back to you.

I have found life is much easier when I say out loud only things that would be OK if that person ever found out I said them. Having a clear conscience is relaxing, and allows me to focus on positive things like my relationships, setting and achieving goals, and taking care of myself.

If gossip or judgment is common for you, get out of the negative loop. If you have been "programmed" through social norms to gossip about or judge others, it might take some work to un-learn this, but it is well worth the change.

Practice with the people closest to you. When a friend

opens up about hopes, dreams, and fears, recognize it as a precious moment. She is trusting you and making herself vulnerable. No matter how light-hearted and "no big deal" she may appear as she mentions something new in her life, be sure not to squander the trust that can be built in that moment, by passing judgment about what she has said. Rather than giving your opinion about what she tells you, encourage her to share more about it instead. "Wow, tell me more." "What do you think?" "How did this come up?" Then, once you have really understood where she is coming from and you still have a judgment, you can frame it like this. "My concern is _____." This feels much less like a judgment because it is your concern, and you are giving her the choice if she wants to take it as her concern too, or not.

And as far as letting go of judging others, do a check at the end of the day, "Did I say anything about anyone today that I would not be happy for that person to hear?"

REFLECTION QUESTIONS

What is my main saboteur and in which situations does it show up?

How can I begin to notice when my saboteur is "in charge"? Who can help me?

What changes would I make in my life if I were not at all afraid of consequences?

The Four Channels of Confidence

Think of a current challenge you face; if you were guaranteed success, what would be your next step?

3. THE VOICE CHANNEL

The Voice Channel of confidence is often the first indication we have of someone's level of confidence. When you have been nervous giving a presentation, have you ever heard your own voice shake or tremble? Have you gotten feedback that you speak too quietly or too loudly? The more we notice these things, the more nervous we become, and it can be a vicious cycle.

What message is your voice sending? Does it send a message of confidence that you're happy with? Or is it projecting a level of confidence that's lower than you would like? Is your voice loud enough to be heard? Is it overly loud? Do you take responsibility for making yourself heard?

Like our body, our voice is an instrument. And it's a shame how little we practice using it to our advantage. We can become more aware of our voice and using it as a channel of confidence by paying attention to our tone of voice, our range of speaking styles and volumes, and also through the words we choose.

A confident voice is strong, clear, easy to understand, and just the right volume. We can use our Voice Channel to create a confident message by avoiding "filler" words like ums and ahs, and when we speak accurately or "impeccably", as Don Miguel Ruiz explains in his excellent book, The Four Agreements.[16] We show our confidence by the way our voices sound, and we can feel more confident if we hear ourselves speaking more confidently.

I once ran a leadership development program in which singer and renowned vocal coach Monika Ballwein was a guest speaker. She spoke to a group of managers, most of whom had never had voice coaching, and helped some incredibly soft-spoken, reserved people sound confident and outgoing. The first thing she said was, "Your voice can be like a Ferrari, but most people drive theirs like a Fiat."[17] She meant that we use a very limited range of volume, pitch, and style in our voices. Our voices are often an underutilized resource.

VOLUME, PITCH, AND TONE OF VOICE

Imagine your voice is like a piano keyboard; it has 88 keys, but most of us use only ten to twenty of those keys. I

---

[16] (Ruiz 1997)
[17] (Ballwein.com 2014)

have worked with many people who receive feedback from me, or others, that they are too monotone. Some of them try to vary their voices, but their attempts are so small that they hardly make a difference. So I ask them, "What makes it difficult to start varying your voice and trying out some of these techniques?"

They say, "I feel like I am varying it a lot already," or "If I do any more, I'm afraid I'm going to sound stupid," or "I'm going to sound fake or like a clown." However, they can't hear themselves like others can.

Most people don't realize the impact that their voices can have, because they have never experimented with the different things their voices can do. Think about voices that you've heard in your life: on TV, in person, or on video clips. What do uncertain voices sound like? They usually are very low in volume and the words are often mumbled, or they are inappropriately loud and/or talking too fast. Now think about the people who are confident. There is something about their volume; it is louder than less-confident people, but not necessarily overly loud. Somehow, those voices are easier to understand. The volume is just right to be able to hear them without feeling like they are yelling. They don't seem to have any reason to hide what they are saying. When people feel confident about what they have to say, they make sure that others can hear them. If we are subconsciously afraid of being judged for what we say, we may tend to get it over with quickly by speaking fast, or aim to not be heard by speaking softly.

Think about yourself in any recent group discussion. When you feel like you have the right answer, you speak in a way that you know people will hear you. However, if you're not sure of yourself, you may say things in a lower voice. That way, if they hear and it's correct, then you have nothing to worry about; but if they don't hear it and it was the wrong answer, then you won't risk feeling embarrassed. Somehow, this feels safer. However, it is also potentially self-sabotaging to your confidence, because if people do not hear your contribution, then someone else may bring up the same idea and receive all the credit. Or worse, your saboteur may convince you that people heard you and purposefully ignored you or shunned your idea.

The most-confident women are comfortable being heard, being wrong, and being willing to be corrected and learn. They would rather make a mistake than share ideas in a half-hearted manner. Again, confidence is not just about speaking louder. Sometimes the least-confident people are overly loud because they are uncomfortable, and feel it is the only way to be heard.

A confident voice is also the right pitch—usually lower rather than higher. Moreover, sadly for women, who physiologically tend to have higher voices than men, there are studies that show that people have a bias to prefer and believe people who have lower voices.[18] That being said, we can take action to at least use the full lower end of our own voice's spectrum.

Sometimes when we're nervous, we tense up, and part of this tension is held in our throat, which means our voice will be at a higher-than-natural pitch. The level of tension in our muscles is what makes the difference between that nervous high-pitched voice and a more relaxed voice.

If you feel nervous or insecure, take a moment to pay attention to your neck and throat muscles. Take a deep breath and relax them as much as possible. It is very simple if you are conscious of it. Before an important meeting or presentation, you can relax the muscles in your throat by doing neck rolls, vocal warm-up exercises like singing scales; humming also relaxes your throat muscles, as does drinking warm beverages.

Monika Ballwein also talked about the color of sound. You can speak with "dark" sound color, when you make more space in your mouth, so it sounds dark and airy. You can produce a light voice when your mouth and throat have less space. Compare it with a clap; more space between your hands means darker sound color, less

---

18

https://papers.ssrn.com/sol3/papers.cfm?abstract_id=4168777#:~:text=We%20first%20demonstrate%20a%20strong,between%20men%20than%20women%20candidates
https://macsphere.mcmaster.ca/bitstream/11375/15438/1/Tigue_Cara_C_201405_PhD.pdf

space (clapping with flat hands) means lighter sound color. Your voice is equipped with an incredible range. You can choose. It is not only black and white; a whole spectrum of color can help you vary how you communicate your message.

In summary, it's about experimenting, practicing, and finding ways that you haven't been using your voice until now. Next time you are in the shower, practice making your voice darker or lighter, or practice seeing the difference when you tighten or relax your throat. Give yourself the opportunity to start playing on more keys of the keyboard.

SPEED AND PAUSES

The speed of your voice is also an area to keep an eye on. Most of us talk much more quickly than we realize. The hardest part is recognizing that we are speaking too fast in the first place. The best way to learn, is to ask for feedback from others. That's a universal rule for personal development: get feedback so you can improve. Practice does not make perfect, practice makes comfortable. Practice plus feedback is what really helps us improve. An exercise you can do on your own is to exaggerate how slowly you speak. Say the first few lines of an upcoming speech as slowly as you can. Close your eyes and imagine someone who had just learned your language is listening. Make sure you pronounce every syllable clearly and thoroughly. It may feel funny to do this, but it is helpful to practice the range of speed and level of enunciation you are capable of.

You can detect when people are not confident, not only by low volume, high pitch, and high speed, but also by whether or not their voices tremor. When people are nervous, their voices may shake. It's happened to me many times, my voice shaking slightly during an interview or on stage. However, this is also something we can remedy. This is where the fundamental tool of breathing comes in again. To raise the volume and steadiness of your voice, you need to have breath behind it. Picture the lungs like a bagpipe. The bagpipe must have enough air in it to make a noise. When your lungs are empty and you attempt to say something loud, it's quite difficult, and your voice shakes. Now breathe in and with full lungs, say something loud.

Go ahead, I dare you to do it right now. "Say something loud!"

Now, take a full breath in and then, "Say something loud!" again. Notice how much easier it is to be loud? When you have full lungs, you naturally can speak loudly, with no tremors. Your breath and your voice work in combination. To have a strong voice, you need to breathe properly, and to breathe properly, you need to be sitting up straight, so your diaphragm isn't constricted. And surprise, surprise, when you sit up straight, you will look and start to feel more confident! All these elements are connected!

Pauses are also a sign of confidence, and an opportunity to think and breathe. Don't be afraid of silence! Many people are afraid that if they wait too long to answer a question, they will look ill prepared, or even stupid. If you have ever heard an interview with Elon Musk, you might have noticed he pauses sometimes for ten seconds or more, after being asked a particularly tough question. He uses the chance to think and construct his answer before he begins to speak. Not many people have the courage to hold silence like that.

Silence is our friend (as mentioned in the Breath Channel chapter). I have noticed that, surprisingly, it is one of the best ways to ensure you have an audience's attention. Try it—next time you are giving a presentation, pause for four or five seconds. You will see that people whose eye contact has wandered away, will look up to see what is happening. Suddenly, you have their attention again, and you can continue talking with renewed confidence that people are really listening. Monotonous, non-stop speech can start to act like white noise for an audience, lulling them to sleep. Think of silence as part of your vocabulary.

The best part about being able to build pauses into your speech pattern? While you are silent, you have a chance to breathe more deeply, which in turn calms your nervous system and helps you have access to your full brain.

STRONG WORDS

Your choice of words is also part of the Voice Channel. Do you find yourself saying, um, like, or sort of, over and over again when you are talking? These are called filler words, and they take away from the effectiveness of your speech. They are distracting and a missed opportunity to stop and breathe.

The way your voice sounds reveals your confidence level, and the Voice Channel is one way that you can increase your impact. By using a greater range of voice, supported by proper breathing and pauses, you convey your point more effectively. Once you take the steps to breathe and support your voice properly, your self-assuredness will also get a boost, creating a virtuous cycle.

REFLECTION QUESTIONS

What does my voice convey currently? Confidence? Nerves? Something else?

What is the best way to experiment with more range in the volume, speed and pitch of my voice?

What can I do to prepare my voice for important presentations and meetings?

4. THE BODY CHANNEL

Most people neglect their bodies. I know I did, for many years. It was essentially just a tripod for my head. As long as my body did what it is supposed to do, I would ignore it. I thought paying attention to your body was only for athletes. But I learned that my body is also an instrument. Not only that, but it is one way that projects how we view ourselves. It shows on the outside what we put on the inside through our physical appearance, and it shows how we feel about ourselves through our posture. Our body not only reveals how confident we feel, but actually can be a source of confidence in and of itself.

Our body is where we feel our emotions, and emotions are valuable data. If we listen to our body, it will tell us if a situation is OK or not. Haven't you ever had a bad feeling in your gut when you agreed to something you were not actually comfortable with? Did you ever experience the visceral reaction of being insulted or left out? Our body is trying to tell us something in those moments. We need to learn to listen to the signals our body sends us. To feel confident, we need to check in with our body before we start a new activity.

When you start to get stressed, your body tells you so. Your heart rate starts to rise, and your palms start sweating. This is a gift, actually! A lot of us think, "I can't stand it when I start sweating and can feel my heart pounding. It distracts me. It's a real problem." However, it is a gift if our heart rate rises. It's a signal to say, "OK, I need to pause a minute and make a shift." That shift could be as simple as sitting up straighter, uncrossing your legs, taking some deeper breaths, bringing your focus to the present moment, remembering your personal mantra, or noticing the saboteur voice.

THE FOUNDATIONS

Think of a time when you felt confident in your life; I can imagine it was not on a day when you felt sick and tired. There is so much to be said for maintaining the foundations of health to be at your most confident. I have met many people who are struggling with not only low confidence, but also problems such as low motivation, interpersonal conflict, stress, irritability, and anxiety, and are looking for tools and tips to "fix" those problems. All of these topics can be exacerbated when we are not at our best physically. Underlying fatigue or the roller-coaster ride of sugar highs and lows can make it very difficult to regulate our emotions. We are particularly susceptible to the saboteur voice when we are tired, or have spikes in blood sugar. Before you start with any fancy new habits, I believe it is wise to make sure your foundations are in place first.

SLEEP: Are you averaging 7.5-8 hours a night?

HYDRATION: Do you drink at least 2 liters (65oz) of water a day?

NUTRITION: Is the majority of your food vegetables and whole grains, and do you avoid processed food and sugar, including sugary drinks and sweets?

MOVEMENT: Do you do at least some light exercise every day?

BREATHING: Do you spend at least five minutes a day doing breathing exercises, mindfulness, or meditation?

Without these foundations in place, it is very hard to have a constant level of energy, and without energy, it is hard to feel confident. We are meant to feel energetic all day long. We do not need to fight fatigue while we are working. If you struggle with fatigue or irritability, double-check your foundations. As an experiment, do whatever it takes to be able to check all five boxes every day for at least two weeks, and see what happens!

If you are struggling with sleeping enough, you may need to skip Netflix and late-evening working sessions. Stopping eating at least two hours before bed, helps your body not have to choose between digestion and rest and repair of your cells. Sleep is also the time when our brain processes the emotional events of the day, which is why it is so much harder to manage your emotions when you have not slept enough.

I have a sleep tracker, which lets me know exactly how much I have rested. Through that I have seen what impacts my sleep negatively, like alcohol or late working. I have learned that I need about 90 minutes after I am done with my daily work and family duties, to really wind down before bed. That means, starting my own bedtime routine pretty much directly after I put my son to bed. Of course, I cannot always manage this, but when I do, I sleep better and notice I am much more confident the next day.

In the morning as I am making coffee, I have made it a habit to drink one liter of water. This already gets me halfway to my water goal. Because I do not drink juice or soda and it is pretty much effortless to drink a second liter of water over the course of the day, since every time I am thirsty, I drink water.

I have experimented with many different food regimens, and I have found that I am most energetic and confident when I cut out processed sugar all together. That means reading labels on everything I buy. I also am at my best when I eat only wholewheat bread and flour, and no white flour products. I also practice time-restricted eating, which entails giving my body a 14–16-hour break from food in every 24-hour period. I have noticed when I do these things my thinking is sharper, my mood is more stable, and I do not have any dips in energy throughout the day.

Of course, I do not manage to have all these foundations in place all the time. We all get thrown off from routines and habits, for many reasons. Self-awareness, self-honesty and self-compassion are key (and a lot harder than they seem). What I have realized, is how important it is to check in with myself to see how I am feeling. If it is anything other than confident, I ask myself if my foundations are in place. Usually in those moments, they are not, and I must go back to the basics. I aim to do so without listening too much to the saboteur, who would love to berate me in that moment. Curiosity rather than self-judgment makes it much easier to hit the reset button on bad habits and reinstate the foundation. For example, "Interesting, I started working late again, I wonder what prompted that?" Or, "Look at that, I seem to have a hard time resisting sweets again, did something change?"

The chain reaction can happen like this: I went to bed late last night because I couldn't just leave that cliff-hanger on Netflix. I was tired this morning and that frappuccino just looked so good, I couldn't resist. Two hours later, I was getting "hangry" because my blood sugar plummeted, and so I snapped at my colleague. Then we went into our sales meeting, and I felt really defensive about my numbers because that colleague was asking questions I couldn't answer. My confidence was rock bottom by lunch.

Usually, there is a link to one or another part of the foundation that is not in place. You have to be honest with yourself, forgive yourself, and go back to basics.

It is easy to miss the connection between the foundations and confidence. After all, it is normalized in our society to binge-watch, sleep too little, work too much, eat junk food and drink soda. But once you have the experience of having a solid physical foundation and see how much easier it is to handle stress and challenging situations, then you will always have an anchor for your confidence.

POSTURE

Picture a confident person that you know. What is their body posture like? Shoulders slumped? Hands shoved in pockets with elbows folded in? Probably not.

Posture is one of the quickest and simplest things we can do to feel and look more confident. Confident body posture is shoulders back, long spine, and balanced weight on both legs or sit bones.

Are you sitting up straight with your shoulders back? If not, then do it now. Posture is the "low-hanging fruit" of confidence: easy to do, easy to check, for free, and available to you at any time of day.

Imagine you are on stage in a choir. You have practiced for months and are excited about tonight's performance. You feel confident about your singing voice and know that your voice is important. How would you stand? Close your eyes for a second, imagine the scene and take on this posture. How does it feel? This is likely your most confident body posture.

Now imagine you are sitting in a chair and suddenly you hear gunshots ring out. You are not sure if you are in the line of fire or not. What do you do with your body if you can't run or get out of your chair? Do it now. Chances are you make yourself as small as possible.

Notice how close this body posture is to how we hold our body when we are sitting in a waiting room and texting on our phones.

Many years ago, I signed up for a course on how to learn to walk in stiletto shoes. I was surprised to find out that 75% of the course was about posture. That's because if you're going to wear sexy shoes like stilettos, you have to own it, you've got to work it, you have to walk in a way that shows that you're not afraid to be seen.

Part of confidence is not hiding. So here are three tips on how to hold your body in a way that projects confidence.

1. **Back straight.** We know we're supposed to sit up

straight and stand up straight, but we sometimes forget. Find a way to remind yourself multiple times during the day to straighten up again.

2. **Shoulders back.** Those muscles between your shoulder blades don't get enough work. If we hold our shoulders back, the unspoken message we are sending is: we don't have anything to hide and have nothing to fear. It shows that you're open and comfortable with yourself, not feeling the need to hide or be small.

3. **String from your head.** Imagine a string connecting the crown of your head to the ceiling. In this posture, your eyes should be trained directly in front of you. From this position it is natural to make eye contact, and harder to look at the ground. This makes it easier for you to make a connection with people, and you will appear more confident. It will also keep your neck comfortable and relaxed, something that's very important, as I learned in later years from physical therapists, to prevent neck pain. Who can feel confident when they're in pain?

Adjust your posture any time to give yourself an internal boost in confidence, and you will also project more confidence externally.

NERVOUS SYSTEM

Research from Amy Cuddy and her colleagues at Harvard and Columbia University, has found that the levels of cortisol and testosterone in our blood impact our feelings of confidence.[19] The adrenal gland produces the hormone cortisol when it believes it will need a large metabolic output, in response to stress. It generates energy to prepare for exertion or dealing with threats. It puts our body in a heightened, reactive state. Testosterone, on the other hand, is a hormone that reflects and reinforces feelings of status and dominance. It generates feelings of confidence and risk tolerance.

Men and women alike feel more confident when we have higher levels of testosterone coursing through our veins. Levels of testosterone in our blood rise in anticipation of a competition, and also after a victory. The converse is true after a perceived defeat. We are more willing to take risks when the levels of testosterone in our blood are high. No wonder our confidence goes down after losing, and no wonder we often find it hard to get back on the horse and try again.

When I first learned that increased testosterone helps contribute to confidence, I thought, "Great, I'm supposed to have testosterone? What does that mean—that I have to grow hair on my chest to feel confident?" Of course, I was associating testosterone with men. It is in fact the male sex hormone, and estrogen is the female sex hormone. However, men and women have both estrogen and testosterone in their systems. Fortunately, increasing our level of confidence requires only a tiny boost of

---

[19] (Carney, Cuddy, and Yap 2010)

testosterone. Don't worry; we won't become manly if we boost the testosterone in our systems. The fact that the male sex hormone encourages feelings of confidence, makes it no surprise that a so-called confidence gap exists between men and women. We're built that way! Yet, we have many healthy, simple, and fast ways to increase our body's sense of confidence.

We can impact the levels of cortisol and testosterone in our blood. In her TED talk,[20] Cuddy explains that the ways we hold our physical bodies actually send a message to our brains, that tells our bodies to produce either cortisol or testosterone. High-power poses increase testosterone and lower cortisol, and low-power poses do the opposite.

High-power poses are those body positions that take up space—positions that make us feel strong. They include putting your feet up on the desk, or leaning back with your hands crossed behind your head. Another is standing like Wonder Woman with your legs straight, feet solidly on the ground, and fists on your hips. Cuddy also refers to power poses in the animal kingdom, such as when peacocks spread their feathers, or cobras open their hoods. These poses not only display dominance, they actually create a feeling of dominance. This is true in humans, too.

Cuddy also shares the phenomenon that when humans experience victory, they tend to raise both arms in the air

---

[20] (Cuddy 2012)

in the shape of a V. Even blind people who were born without sight, do this when they win something great. Although they have never actually seen anyone pose that way, it is a natural response to that feeling of victory. Power posing is an instinctual part of our human makeup.

Conversely, we also have what Cuddy calls low-power poses. With these body positions, we are closed up or making ourselves small. For example, crossing our legs, crossing our arms, touching our neck, and folding up, all manage to make us seem smaller. I can't help but notice that these low-power poses are very similar to the "ladylike" behavior women are encouraged to learn as adolescents (e.g., cross your legs when you sit, keep your hands folded, rest your hands on your lap). We are certainly not encouraged to drape an arm over the chair next to us or take up lots of space. I am not saying we should burn our bras and start sitting with our legs wide apart (aptly named "manspreading"), but I do think it is important to recognize those moments when we need to bolster our confidence, and check to make sure we aren't overly "folded up" physically in that moment.

When we hold our bodies in low-power positions, we are signaling to our brains that we're not safe, and that we need to protect ourselves. In turn, the body creates cortisol, which makes us feel under threat. Cortisol is not an "evil" hormone. It has its time and its place. Together with adrenaline, it helps us respond to challenges, and tells the body to prepare for threats. Cortisol triggers a higher heart rate, higher blood pressure, and more perspiration, because it is telling the body, "You may need to protect yourself!" It has an important function, but when it remains elevated over time, it has been linked to stress-related illnesses[21] and lowered self-confidence. Elevated levels of cortisol in the blood are linked to a whole host of nasty complications, such as increased chances of osteoporosis,[22] loss of collagen in the skin,[23] increased blood pressure,[24] negative impact on fertility,[25] and many others.

In short, we should make it top priority to keep our cortisol levels low when we do not actually face a large metabolic output. How? There are many ways besides just holding power poses and taking deep breaths, including massage therapy,[26] music therapy,[27] laughing,[28] taking a walk,[29] and dancing[30].

No wonder so many of us love those things! Who would have thought getting a massage might contribute to your confidence?

The key is to be aware what messages we are sending to our brain, by what we do with our body. There are so

---

[21] (Mayo Clinic Staff 2014)
[22] (Knight, Kornfeld, Glaser, and Bondy 1955)
[23] (Kucharz 1987)
[24] (Kennedy 2014)
[25] (Nelson 2011)
[26] (Field, Hernandez-Reif, Diego, Schanberg, and Kuhn 2005)
[27] (Uedo et al. 2003)
[28] (Berk, Tan, and Berk 2008)
[29] (Starks, Starks, Kingsley, Purpura, and Jäger 2008)
[30] (Quiroga Murcia, Bongard, and Kreutz 2009)

many simple shortcuts, it's incredible how little we use them. I know many people who watch Cuddy's TED talk, but still don't take the time to do what she recommends, such as hold a power pose for two minutes in preparation for a stressful situation. It takes only two minutes!

I was able to use these tips recently during a tennis tournament. I love tennis and being on the court, but sports have always been a sensitive topic. As a child, I was the slowest in the race and the last to be picked for the team. My saboteur has clung on to these experiences, and likes to bring them out when I decide to challenge myself athletically.

One year, I did just that by entering a tennis tournament. I was shocked at how difficult it was to keep my confidence out of the gutter. I underestimated the emotional impact of a formal competition. So I decided to stand in a Wonder Woman position every single chance I got. Between points, during breaks, and when changing sides, I would stand or walk with my fists on my hips (racket in one hand), take deep slow breaths from my stomach and focus on sounds I heard and sensations I felt at that moment in order to be present. The positive impact it had on my game was incredible!

Your physical health, posture and nervous system are all either supporting or hindering your confidence. In order to increase the chances of feeling confident, make sure you are treating your body well, sit up straight, and make sure you are in a power-neutral position (not making yourself small). Be aware of the impact of how you hold your body.

REFLECTION QUESTIONS

What can I do to strengthen the foundations for my physical health?

What is the best way for me to check in with my emotions and my body to gauge how I really feel about a situation?

What can I do to improve my posture generally?

How can I remember to use power pose exercises before important meetings or presentations?

MULTIPLYING YOUR CONFIDENCE THROUGH RELATIONSHIPS

What do strong relationships have to do with confidence? We do not operate in a vacuum. Our confidence very much depends on how we respond to the people and situations around us. Researchers have found that positive social relationships, social support and social acceptance help shape the development of self-esteem in people over time across ages four to 76. There is also a significant effect in the reverse direction.[31]

Moreover, chances are, you are not the only one in your circle of friends who would like to increase their level of confidence. What can we do to support our friends' confidence?

Be there for them when they are down, not just when it is easy. It is not your job to "fix" their

---
[31] (Harris and Orth 2016)

low confidence, but to listen to them without judgment. Be sure to ask what the person needs at any one moment. For example, ask them, "How can I support you best right now? Just listen? Give you my opinion?"

Point out their strengths and attributes when you see them in action. Sometimes the things we excel at just feel normal to us. "Doesn't everybody type this fast?" "Doesn't everybody know how to tell a story?" You can say things like, "Wow, you are really good at dealing with stressful driving situations!" "Did you know you are excellent at explaining things?" "Your downward dog pose looks exactly like the teacher's!" Knowing our strengths can help us boost our Attitude Channel, by being the basis of a mantra or an antidote to our saboteur voice.

Give feedback. Although feedback can be hard to take sometimes, when it comes from a loving friend who has the intention to help you, it can give a huge boost to your confidence in the long term. "Your voice was strong and clear and your eye contact with the audience was consistent. This gave you a lot of credibility on stage. And, your shoulders were slumped, so it undermined your confidence. Don't forget to keep your shoulders back next time!"

Do activities together that make you both feel good. Instead of going for cocktails after work every time you meet, mix it up and go for a walk sometimes instead. Ask each other to join classes and events that support confidence building, like breathing exercises, yoga or Pilates for posture, meditation, voice training, or workshops to identify strengths.

Call them when you need help. When I ask a group of women, "Who likes to help others?" 90% of hands go up. And when I ask, "Who here likes to ask for help?" usually only one or two hands go up. So how are all these people who like to help others going to get the chance to help, if no one ever asks for it? Chances are, they will "help" in situations where they think help is needed, even if it is not. This can create all sorts of other problems—enough to fill another book. Wouldn't you hate to imagine that your best friend felt reluctant to ask you for help? Be the role model, show her what it looks like to ask for help and that it is OK. And, bonus, you get the help you need!

Make a confidence pact with your best friends. Commit to calling each other out when someone makes a negative statement about herself or anybody else. Building your own confidence, is supported by being kind to others as well. Make an effort to notice what people are doing well, when they look great, when they are making an effort, and say it out loud. This will train your brain to be more positive, to get used to looking for what is working, instead of what is not. And this, in turn, will slowly erode the saboteur's power.

Focus on others instead of being down on yourself. Have you ever noticed how easy it is to snap out of a bad mood if someone around you needs help? But you don't have to wait until someone needs help to focus on others. There is always opportunity to give the people in our lives more attention. This helps us get out of our heads, especially if we are ruminating about something. And if you don't have many relationships, sign up to volunteer. There are always people in need and opportunities to connect with others.

Our friendships are gifts. Make sure you surround yourself with people who boost your confidence, not undermine it. Ask yourself how you feel after spending time with each friend, and do your best to increase time with the ones who make you feel good, and decrease time with the others. Share the above with your friends and see if they are willing to do these things for you. Then nurture those friendships!

FINAL VISUALIZATION AND REFLECTION

Learning what you transmit to the outside world via your breathing, your attitude, your voice, and your body, is a great way to increase your confidence. Don't be afraid to make an adjustment or two to those channels, to feel more confident from the inside.

At some point while reading, you may have been thinking, "OK, this is not rocket science. I know this stuff already." That's right—this stuff is simple! However, beware: simple is not always easy. The question is, if you know this stuff, why aren't you doing it consistently?

You might need a mental and emotional anchor in order to be able to make a shift. Set aside about ten minutes to do the following exercise.

You may choose to listen to a guided visualization here.

Otherwise, just read the following instructions and go at your own pace.

Close your eyes and take a few deep breaths, and imagine yourself with your new level of confidence. Really picture it. Notice how you feel, what you are wearing, where you are, how people respond to you. Notice the details and get in touch with the feeling.

Stay there in this visualization for as long as you can.

When you open your eyes again, take note of what you experienced.

I hope the Four Channels provide an easy-to-remember framework to capture all of these concepts that are easy to know, but not easy to attend to. Don't forget to continually and regularly check your channels (Breath, Attitude, Voice, and Body). Are you doing everything possible to support yourself in all of them?

Remember the reflection you did at the beginning of this book? I am going to have you set a goal for yourself. Please be patient with yourself. Learning about these tools is just one part of your journey. Now the real work begins!

Now for some more coaching questions, to help you build an action plan for yourself:

You considered yourself at the _____ Stage of Confidence at the beginning of this book. (Cocoon, Dismissal, Dependence, Equanimity) Which of the Four Channels could give you the biggest boost to reach a new stage of confidence?

What stage would you like to achieve one year from now?

What will it feel like for you to be at your goal level of confidence? What would be different in your life?

Which of your strengths can you utilize more to increase your confidence?

What resources or people will you need to call upon to do what you read about in this book?

What new habit will you start tomorrow to increase your confidence?

Once you have answered these questions, set them aside for a few days. Set a reminder to come back and look at those answers again in a few days. Ideally after a morning meditation or walk in nature. This will help you feel at your calmest, when your cortisol levels are low.

Now you are ready to construct an action plan.

YOUR ACTION PLAN

My goal is to have a confidence level of ____ out of 10. I will know I have reached that goal because:

To move in that direction, my first three actions are:

1. I am going to start by

2. I will also

3. And I will

Write down your goals and check back every few months to see how you are doing. To support yourself even more, share your goals with someone who can help hold you accountable, by asking how it is going and giving you feedback.

I am going to ask _____ to support me in reaching my goals. I will speak to this person about this by (date)_____.

I hope you have enjoyed this book. I wish you, as the Italians say, forza e coraggio (strength and courage) for your journey!

Warmly, Margo

REFERENCES

Ballwein.com (2014). CVT Vocal Coach Monika Ballwein. http://www.ballwein.com

Berk, L., Tan, S., and Berk, D. (2008). Cortisol and Catecholamine stress hormone decrease is associated with the behavior of perceptual anticipation of mirthful laughter. FASEB J, 22(1), 946.

Cuddy, Amy (2012) TED Talk, Your body language may shape who you are

Carney, D., Cuddy, A., and Yap, A. (2010). Power Posing: Brief Nonverbal Displays Affect Neuroendocrine Levels and Risk Tolerance (1st ed.). Psychological Science. http://www.people.hbs.edu/acuddy/in%20press,%20carney,%20cuddy,%20&%20yap,%20psych%20science.pdf

Deutsch, E. (1978). [Pathogenesis of thrombocytopenia. 2. Distribution disorders, pseudo-thrombocytopenias]. Fortschritte der Medizin, 96(14), 761–762.

Dolaman, W., Sim, L., and Wang, A. (2010). Quiet Confidence (1st ed.). Georgetown University.

https://blogs.commons.georgetown.edu/aw366/files/Quiet-Confidence_Final.pdf

Field, T., Hernandez-Reif, M., Diego, M., Schanberg, S., and Kuhn, C. (2005). Cortisol Decreases and Serotonin and Dopamine Increase Following Massage Therapy. Int J Neurosci, 115(10), 1397-1413. doi:10.1080/00207450590956459

Harris, M. A., and Orth, U. (2019, September 26). The Link Between Self-Esteem and Social Relationships: A Meta-Analysis of Longitudinal Studies. *Journal of Personality and Social Psychology*.

Hodson, R., and Sullivan, T. (1995). The Social Organization of Work (1st ed., pp. Chapter 3 pg 69). Belmont: Wadsworth Pub. Co.

Kay, K., and Shipman, C, (2014). The Confidence Gap. The Atlantic.

Kelley, T. and Kelley, D. (2014). Creative Confidence by Tom & David Kelley. Creativeconfidence.com. http://www.creativeconfidence.com/

Kennedy, R. (2014). Cortisol (Hydrocortisone). The Doctors Medical Library.

Knight Jr, R., Kornfeld, D., Glaser, G., and Bondy, P. (1955). Effects of Intravenous Hydrocortisone on Electrolytes of Serum and Urine in Man. The Journal of Clinical Endocrinology & Metabolism,15(2), 176–181.

Kucharz, E. (1987). Hormonal control of collagen metabolism. Part II. Endocrinologie, 26(4), 229–237.

Mayo Clinic (2014). Chronic stress puts your health at risk. Mayoclinic.org. http://www.mayoclinic.org/healthy-living/stress-management/in-depth/stress/art-20046037

Melnick, S. (2013). Success under Stress (1st ed.). New York: Amacom.

Merriam-Webster.com. Achilles' heel: Definition and More from the Free Merriam-Webster Dictionary. http://www.merriam-webster.com/dictionary/achilles'%20heel

Merriam-Webster.com. Egotism: Definition and More from the Free Merriam-Webster Dictionary.

http://www.merriam-webster.com/dictionary/egotism

Merriam-Webster.com. Mantra: Definition and More from the Free Merriam-Webster Dictionary. http://www.merriam-webster.com/dictionary/mantra

Nelson, R. (2011). An introduction to behavioral endocrinology (1st ed.). Sunderland, MA: Sinauer Associates.

Quiroga Murcia, C., Bongard, S., and Kreutz, G. (2009). Emotional and Neurohumoral Responses to Dancing Tango Argentino: The Effects of Music and Partner. Music And Medicine, 1(1), 14-21. doi:10.1177/1943862109335064

Ruiz, M. (1997). The Four Agreements: A Practical Guide to Personal Freedom (A Toltec Wisdom Book).

Soffer, L. (1961). The Human Adrenal Gland (1st ed.). Philadelphia, Lea & Febiger.

Starks, M., Starks, S., Kingsley, M., Purpura, M., and Jäger, R. (2008). The effects of phosphatidylserine on endocrine response to moderate intensity exercise. J Int Soc Sports Nutr, 5(1), 11. doi:10.1186/1550-2783-5-11

The Economist (2013). The Feminist Mystique. http://www.economist.com/news/books-and-arts/21573524-what-must-change-women-make-it-top-feminist-mystique

Uedo, N., Ishikawa, H., Morimoto, K., Ishihara, R., Narahara, H., Akedo, I. et al. (2003). Reduction in salivary cortisol level by music therapy during colonoscopic examination. Hepato-Gastroenterology, 51(56), 451–453.

Whitworth, L., Kimsey-House, K., Kimsey-House, H., and Sandahl, P. (1998). Co-active coaching (1st ed.). Palo Alto, Calif. Davies-Black.

ABOUT THE AUTHOR

Margo McClimans is a certified executive coach and leadership development trainer. Her company, Coaching Without Borders™, has been serving leaders across the globe to develop their leadership skills, confidence and cross-cultural abilities since 2005.

She has personally worked with thousands of managers of 60+ nationalities to develop their leadership skills. Together with her team of coaches, she hopes to improve the lives of 1 million people by making 100,000 bosses better leaders. She also speaks at leadership conferences, and guest lectures at business schools and universities.

<u>www.coachingwithoutborders.com</u>

Margo C. McClimans

The Four Channels of Confidence

Made in the USA
Middletown, DE
04 November 2024